HISTORY MAKERS

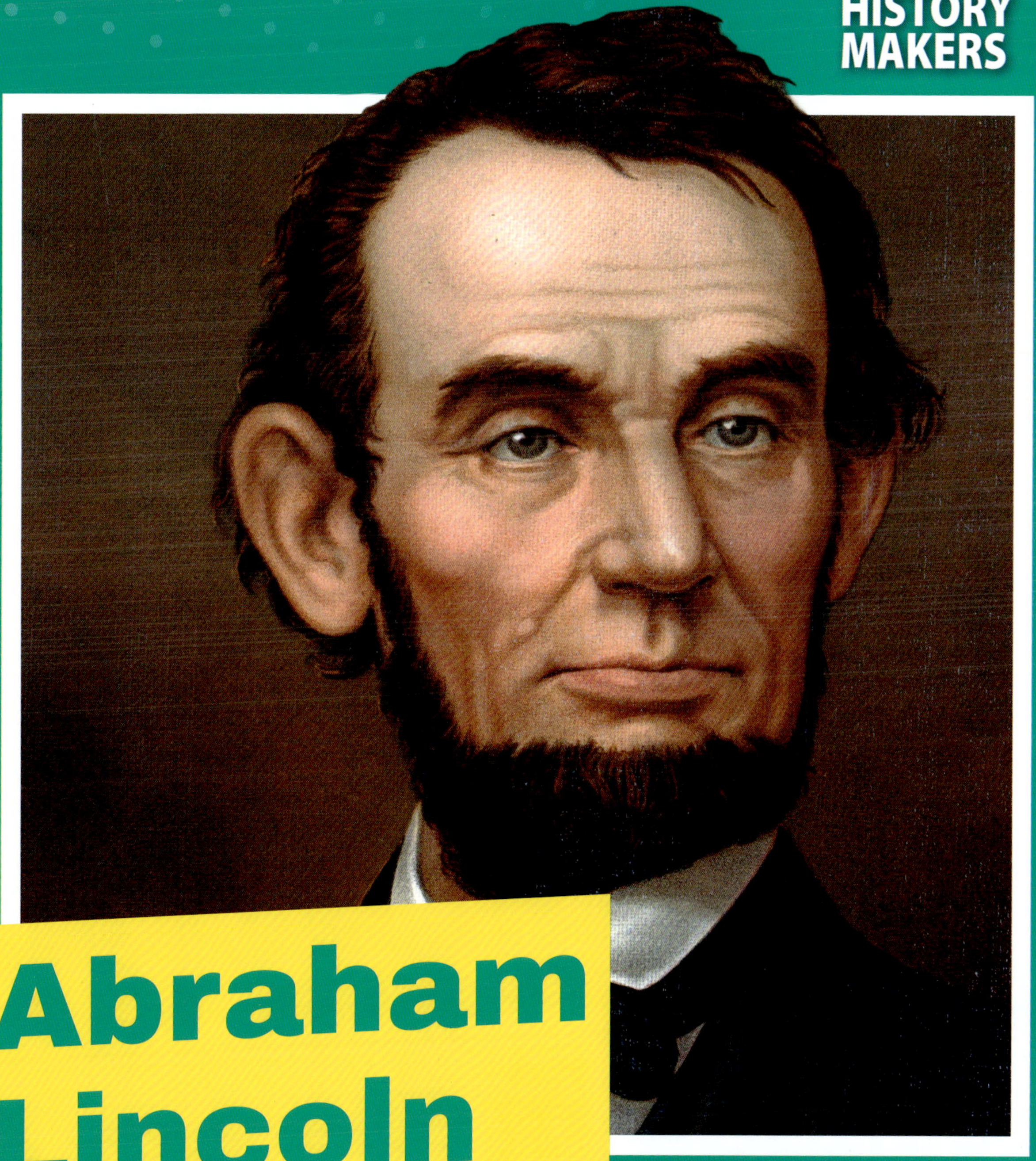

# Abraham Lincoln

Judy Wearing
and Priyanka Das

LIGHTBOX
openlightbox.com

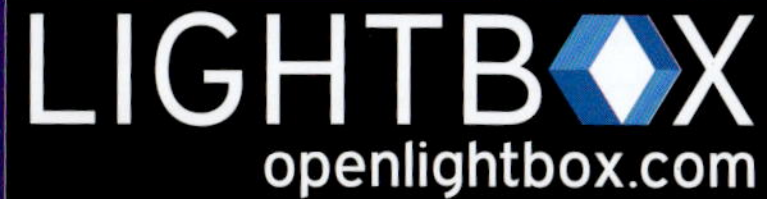

Go to
**www.openlightbox.com**
and enter this book's
unique code.

**ACCESS CODE**

**LBXZ6692**

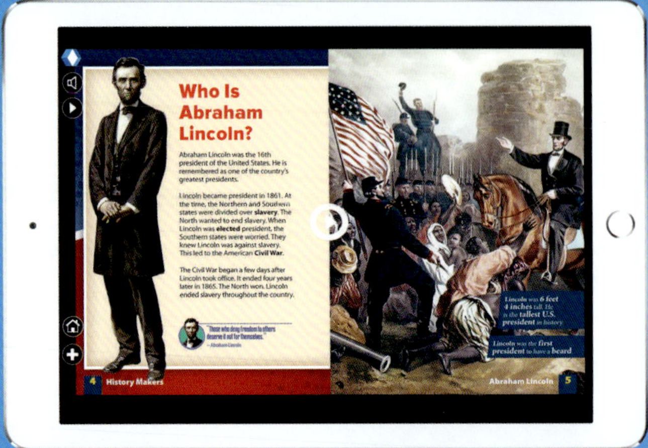


Lightbox is an all-inclusive digital solution for the teaching and learning of curriculum topics in an original, groundbreaking way. Lightbox is based on National Curriculum Standards.

## STANDARD FEATURES OF LIGHTBOX

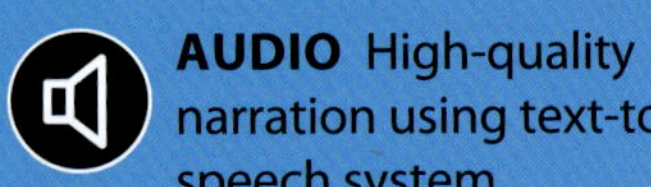
**AUDIO** High-quality narration using text-to-speech system

**ACTIVITIES** Printable PDFs that can be emailed and graded

**SLIDESHOWS** Pictorial overviews of key concepts

**VIDEOS** Embedded high-definition video clips

**WEBLINKS** Curated links to external, child-safe resources

**TRANSPARENCIES** Step-by-step layering of maps, diagrams, charts, and timelines

**INTERACTIVE MAPS** Interactive maps and aerial satellite imagery

**QUIZZES** Ten multiple choice questions that are automatically graded and emailed for teacher assessment

**KEY WORDS** Matching key concepts to their definitions

Copyright © 2020 Smartbook Media Inc. All rights reserved.

# Abraham Lincoln

## CONTENTS

# Who Is Abraham Lincoln?

Abraham Lincoln was the 16th president of the United States. He is remembered as one of the country's greatest presidents.

Lincoln became president in 1861. At the time, the Northern and Southern states were divided over **slavery**. The North wanted to end slavery. When Lincoln was **elected** president, the Southern states were worried. They knew Lincoln was against slavery. This led to the American **Civil War**.

The Civil War began a few days after Lincoln took office. It ended four years later in 1865. The North won. Lincoln ended slavery throughout the country.

"Those who deny freedom to others deserve it not for themselves."

– Abraham Lincoln

Lincoln was **6 feet 4 inches** tall. He is the **tallest U.S. president** in history.

Lincoln was the **first president** to have a **beard**.

# Growing Up

Abraham Lincoln was born on February 12, 1809, in Kentucky. His father, Thomas, was a carpenter and a farmer. Nancy, his mother, was a seamstress.

As a child, Abraham helped the family by gathering wood and carrying water. Abraham and his older sister helped plant the garden.

The Lincolns did not own the land they lived on. When Abraham was eight years old, they were forced to move. The family went to Indiana. They were very poor. The whole family lived in a shack. The land that they settled on was difficult to farm. Abraham helped clear the land and take care of crops.

Lincoln was born in a cabin on a small farm in Hodgenville, Kentucky.

## Get to Know Kentucky

# Influences

Abraham's parents were against slavery. Abraham's mother, Nancy, taught him the importance of kindness. Abraham was kind to others all his life. Nancy died when Abraham was nine years old. It was very hard on him and the family.

Abraham's father married again. Sarah became Abraham's stepmother. She treated Abraham and his sister as her own. Sarah saw that Abraham was eager to learn. She encouraged him and helped him study. With Sarah's help, Abraham taught himself to read.

Sarah remained close to Abraham all his life. He called her "Mother."

The books that Abraham read included *Robinson Crusoe* by Daniel Defoe, *Pilgrim's Progress* by John Bunyan, and Aesop's fables.

# Beginning a Life's Work

Lincoln went to school for only a few months of his life. He studied by reading books at home. When Lincoln's family moved to Illinois, he set out on his own. He worked many jobs. After some time, he became a partner in a general store. He was well known and liked from his time at the store.

After the store failed, Lincoln chose to be a lawyer. He prepared for his exam by reading law books and teaching himself. Lincoln became a lawyer at age 27.

Lincoln decided to try working in **politics**. He wanted to make decisions that would help others. Lincoln was not elected the first time he ran for government. He tried again and won a seat in the Illinois state government in 1834.

Before becoming a lawyer, Lincoln worked as a boatman, a storekeeper, a postmaster, and a surveyor.

**Lincoln's face** is shown on the **one-cent coin** and the **five-dollar bill**.

In **1955**, Illinois adopted **"Land of Lincoln"** as its **state slogan**.

# Overcoming Obstacles

During his life, Lincoln suffered from depression. When he was overcome with sadness, Lincoln found it hard to work. He forced himself to continue, because he knew his work in politics was very important. Lincoln wanted to make a difference to people's lives. He believed that all people should be free.

In 1846, Lincoln was elected to the U.S. House of Representatives. He spoke out against the **Mexican-American War**. He questioned whether or not the United States was right to go to war with Mexico. This made him unpopular with voters. Lincoln decided not to run again. He returned to law.

The Republican Party was formed in 1854 by people who wanted to end slavery. Lincoln joined in 1856. His interest in politics was renewed. He ran for the Senate in 1858. Lincoln lost, but became known for being against slavery. His skill as a **debater** made him famous. It earned him the chance to run for president two years later. Lincoln was elected president in 1860.

Approximately 1,700 U.S. soldiers and 5,000 Mexican soldiers died in battle during the Mexican-American War.

# Achievements and Successes

Lincoln kept the United States together despite the Civil War. Today, he is remembered for ending slavery.

On November 19, 1863, Lincoln gave the Gettysburg Address. It is his most famous speech. Lincoln spoke in Gettysburg, Pennsylvania. This was the site of a major Civil War battle. In the speech, Lincoln talked about the soldiers who took part in the war.

Lincoln also helped set up a bank system in 1863. Everyone in the country began using the same type of money. This helped the **economy** grow.

The Lincoln Memorial is a huge limestone and marble statue of Lincoln. It is in the National Mall in Washington, D.C.

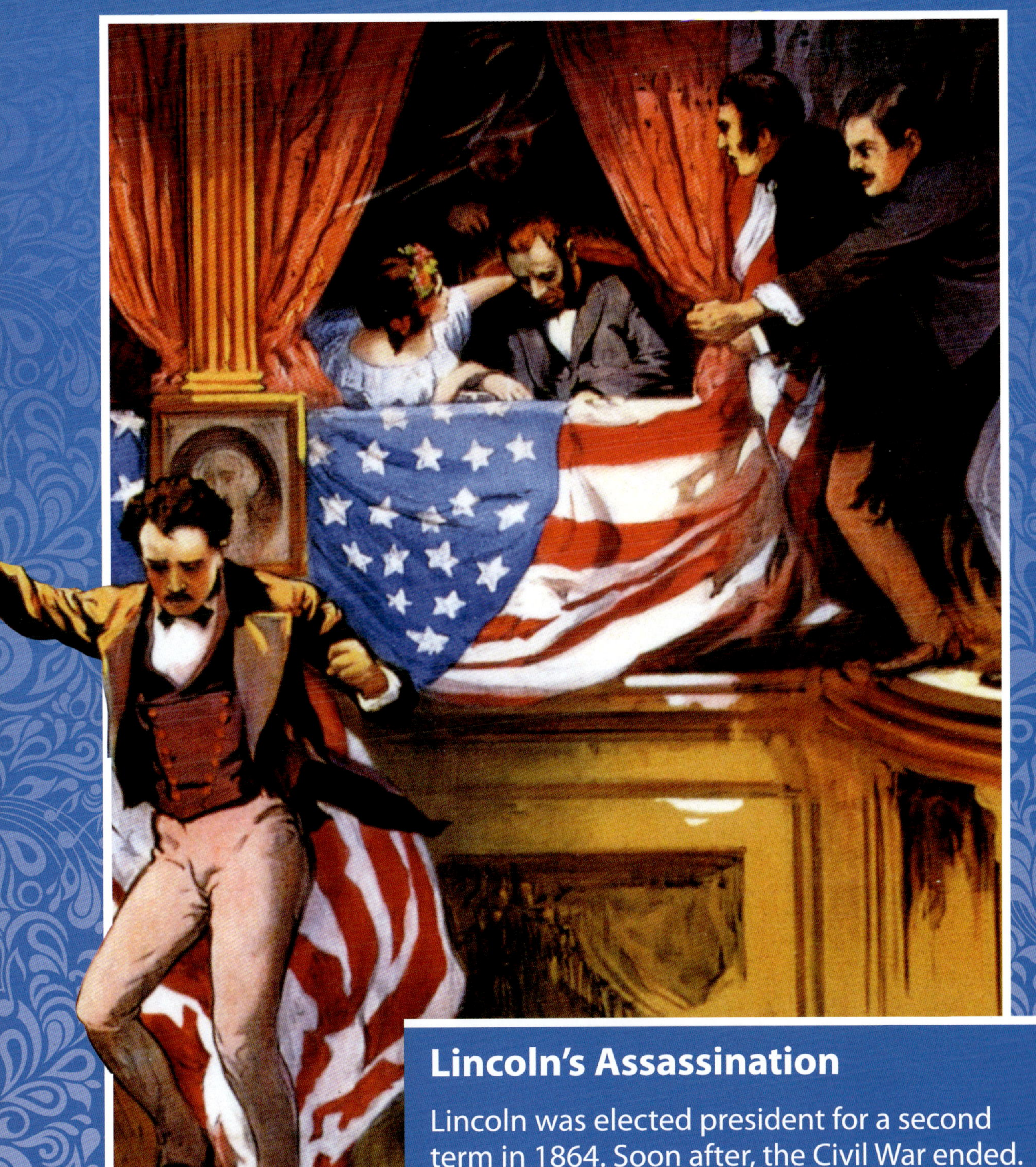

## Lincoln's Assassination

Lincoln was elected president for a second term in 1864. Soon after, the Civil War ended. Five days after the war ended, John Wilkes Booth shot Lincoln as he watched a play. Lincoln was killed. Booth was unhappy that the South had lost the Civil War.

# What Is a President?

The president is the leader of the U.S. government. This person is elected every four years. The people of the United States vote for their leader.

A president leads the country in making important decisions. Many presidents have led the United States through times of crisis. Great presidents have helped shape the country.

Donald Trump is the 45th president of the United States.

# Presidents Through History

Like Lincoln, these presidents overcame obstacles to achieve success.

## George Washington

Washington struggled with spelling and grammar. It is believed that he had **dyslexia**. Despite this, he became the country's first president in 1789. The United States was formed under his leadership. He helped guide the new country's policies.

1789 to 1797

## Thomas Jefferson

Jefferson was the third president of the United States. He did not enjoy giving speeches. Instead, he wrote down his thoughts. At 33 years old, Jefferson wrote the **Declaration of Independence**.

1801 to 1809

## Franklin D. Roosevelt

Roosevelt had a disease called polio. He could not move his legs. Some people thought he should leave politics. Roosevelt did not agree. He continued his political career. In 1932, he was elected president. Roosevelt helped the country through the **Great Depression**. He promised quick action. His message of hope inspired people.

1933 to 1945

## Barack Obama

Obama was the country's first African American president. He was elected in 2008. The country was facing financial difficulties. Obama and his government provided loans to businesses. This helped the businesses to keep running. The economy slowly improved.

2009 to 2017

# ABRAHAM LINCOLN (1809–1865) TIMELINE

**1836**
Lincoln becomes a lawyer.

**1816**
Lincoln's family moves to Indiana.

**1830**
Lincoln's family moves to Illinois. Lincoln makes his first public speech.

**1861**
Lincoln becomes president of the United States. The Civil War begins.

**1863**
Lincoln writes a law to free slaves. However, slavery is not yet ended.

**1864**
Lincoln is re-elected president for a second term.

**1865**
The Civil War ends. The law to free slaves passes. Lincoln is shot on April 14 and dies the next day.

**2019**
A 31-foot statue of Lincoln is installed outside the Abraham Lincoln Presidential Library and Museum in Illinois.

# Write a Biography

A person's life story can be the subject of a book. This kind of book is called a biography. Biographies are often written about people who have achieved great success. These people may have lived many years ago. They may even be alive today. Reading a biography can help you learn more about a great person.

Abraham Lincoln was a great president. Choose another U.S. president and find out more about his life. Learn as much about him as you can. The research outline can guide your research. Read the questions in the outline. Answering these questions will help you write a biography. You can use the internet or books in the library for your research.

## Childhood

- When and where was this person born?
- Describe his family.
- What was his childhood like?

## Main Achievements

- What did he accomplish?
- What awards or recognition has he received?
- How have his achievements served others?
- What makes him a great president?

## Help and Obstacles

- How did he help others?
- What obstacles did he face?
- How did he overcome the obstacles?

# In Your Own Words

What is the correct order of these images? Use each image to help you write Abraham Lincoln's story in your own words.

A

B

C

D

E

F

Answers: 1. E 2. A 3. D 4. F 5. C 6. B

# Key Words

**Civil War:** a war in the United States between the North and South, 1861 to 1865

**debater:** a person who argues about a topic as part of a serious discussion

**Declaration of Independence:** the document written in 1776 that declares the United States free from British rule

**dyslexia:** a condition that makes it hard for a person to read, write, and spell

**economy:** a country's wealth and resources

**elected:** chosen to be a leader in government and to make laws for the people of an area

**Great Depression:** a time in history when many people did not have jobs and most banks closed

**Mexican-American War:** a war between the United States and Mexico over land, 1846 to 1848

**politics:** the work of government and the people who work in government

**slavery:** being owned by another person and not being paid to work

# Index

# LIGHTBOX

## SUPPLEMENTARY RESOURCES

Click on the plus icon found in the bottom left corner of each spread to open additional teacher resources.

- Download and print the book's quizzes and activities
- Access curriculum correlations
- Explore additional web applications that enhance the Lightbox experience

## LIGHTBOX DIGITAL TITLES

### Packed full of integrated media

**VIDEOS**

**INTERACTIVE MAPS**

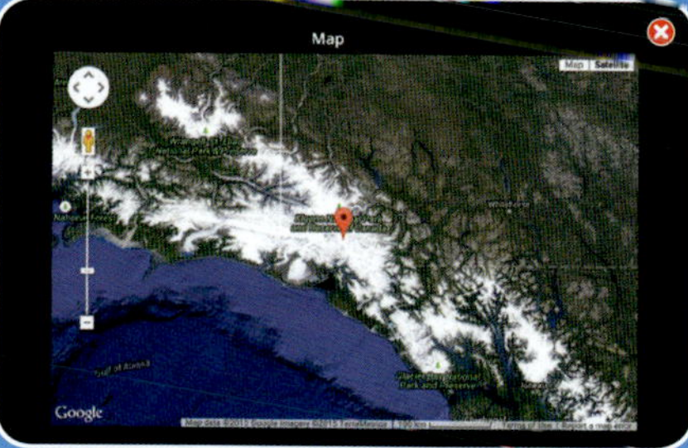


**WEBLINKS**

**SLIDESHOWS**

**QUIZZES**

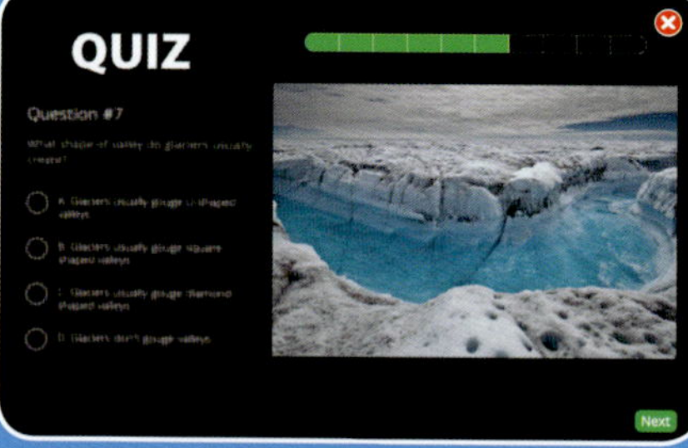


**OPTIMIZED FOR**

- ✔ TABLETS
- ✔ WHITEBOARDS
- ✔ COMPUTERS
- ✔ AND MUCH MORE!

Published by Smartbook Media Inc.
350 5th Avenue, 59th Floor New York, NY 10118
Website: www.openlightbox.com

Copyright © 2020 Smartbook Media Inc.
All rights reserved. No part of this publication may be reproduced, stored in a retrieval system, or transmitted in any form or by any means, electronic, mechanical, photocopying, recording, or otherwise, without the prior written permission of the publisher.

Library of Congress Control Number: 2019939576

ISBN 978-1-5105-4533-5 (hardcover)
ISBN 978-1-5105-4534-2 (multi-user eBook)

Printed in Guangzhou, China
1 2 3 4 5 6 7 8 9 0 23 22 21 20 19

052019
122818

**Project Coordinator:** Priyanka Das
**Art Director:** Terry Paulhus

**Photo Credits**
Every reasonable effort has been made to trace ownership and to obtain permission to reprint copyright material. The publisher would be pleased to have any errors or omissions brought to its attention so that they may be corrected in subsequent printings. The publisher acknowledges Getty Images, iStock, Shutterstock, Alamy, and Bridgeman Images as its primary image suppliers for this title.